A BEGINNER'S GUIDE TO THE SOCRATIC SEMINAR

By
Jerry Chris, Ed.D.

Royal Fireworks Press
Unionville, New York

DEDICATION:

To Patrick Lohmeier and Ryan Elliott, the futures of the active learning process.

Royal Fireworks Press
First Ave, PO Box 399
Unionville, NY 10988
845 726 4444
fax 845 726 3824
email: mail@rfwp.com
website: rfwp.com

ISBN: 978-0-89824-454-0
Printed and bound in the United States of America using soy-based inks on recycled, acid-free paper and environmentally-friendly cover coatings by the Royal Fireworks Printing Company of Unionville, New York.

TABLE OF CONTENTS

CHAPTER 1

General Introduction

The ancient Greeks have been given much of the credit for the creation of the concept of a "Dialogue"—the idea that more could be learned from "thinking together" than could be retained by any form of "didactic" lecturing. Socrates himself, of course, lost his life because, by his own admittance, he encouraged the youth to think rather than simply to memorize. Few societies since Socrates, it seems, other than certain Native American cultures, have fully utilized this method of free-flowing interchange as a means of growth and understanding.

The American educational system, as its methodologies become dictated more and more by standardized tests, and as its teachers become driven more and more by the threat of some form of merit pay based on those tests, seems to be entrenched in the demand for memorization and regurgitation rather than by the love of true learning. When teachers do manage to escape the need to "instruct" – a word which literally means "pour in—they might allow for some "discussion"—which has the same roots as *percussion* and *concussion*, both of which imply a thrusting back and forth of ideas until a winner is determined (Senge).

As all brain research indicates, this is not the way to long-term memory. This is not the way to understanding; this is the means only to short-term retention—just long enough to get the grade on Friday's exam or to pass an Advanced Placement test at the end of the school year, before it is forgotten forever. To be retained for any significant length of time, the material must be learned by *active* involvement—by student ownership of the learning. *Passive*, teacher driven instruction, as is so common now, works only for short-term memory.

A perfect, but sad, illustration of this tragedy comes from a recent attempt at a school I observed to assign particular days to particular subjects for testing. For example, History could only test on Wednesday and Monday; Science on Thursday and Tuesday; Math on Friday and Tuesday; etc. The idea was to prevent students from having to take six exams on the same day (usually Friday). It would have been a bit of an inconvenience for the teachers, but a huge help to the students. However, many teachers objected, led by the Social Science department. Their position was expressed by their chairperson: "*If we finish a unit on Thursday and can't test until Monday, how do you expect the students to remember the answers?*"

Sad indeed. Embarrassing! So let us turn to a positive answer—the Socratic Seminar, which employs *dialogue* as its fundamental methodology. Mortimer Adler, in his "Paideia Proposal" [Paideia literally means "nurturing the whole child"] suggests taking one entire day per week for nothing but Socratic Seminars (Adler). His followers, the Paideia community, foresee the future of classical education as follows:

Didactic Instruction 15 - 20% of classroom time
(lecture)

Coached Projects 60 – 70%
(essays, experiments, math problems, etc.)

Socratic Seminar 15 – 20% (Roberts)

If indeed the Socratic Seminar is to play such a significant role in the classroom, the time has come for all teachers to enter it in their bag of tricks. It is important to note that I suggest a "bag of tricks" and that the Socratic Seminar becomes just one part of it. When I student taught 37 years ago, my master teachers believed that 20 minutes was about the maximum time that students could focus on one activity. Therefore, every class had to have at least two activities. I have heard a variety of experts now suggest that 30 seconds (the length of a TV commercial) is the longest any student can stay glued to the lesson before drifting off to prom dates, the football game, etc. If that is true, the modern teacher does, in fact, need a huge "bag of tricks" and Socratic Seminar can only be one part of it. Therefore, **this book does not** in any way suggest that teachers throw out debate, discussion, etc., but rather that they **add** Socratic Seminar to their repertoire of activities.

One final note should be made by way of general introduction. Somewhere in our attempt to identify gifted students and raise test scores, we have forgotten that the American public school system was designed to be egalitarian—to provide equal opportunity for all. Ideally, the Socratic Seminar does just that; all learners, including the teacher, become equals. Whether the student is an at-risk adolescent, an English Language Learner (ELL), or a gifted prodigy, all have equal voice in the Seminar. And surprisingly, perhaps, all will have equally valuable things to say. We have often purposely mixed these three "categories" of students, and I will readily attest that quite often, in the Seminar format, it is difficult to tell the difference. Labels are just that; they have little relevance to the potential for insight!

CHAPTER 2

Fundamental Differences between Dialogue and Debate

To begin, we must distinguish between "Dialogue," as is used in the Socratic Seminar, and "Debate," as is most commonly employed in our daily interchanges, classroom discussion, dinner conversations, and social repartee.

Dialogue	Debate
Purpose is to understand others' viewpoints	Purpose is to prove others wrong
Requires listening for further meaning	Requires listening to find flaws
Demands an open-mind	Demands prejudgment
Looks for strength in all positions	Looks for weaknesses in opposition's position
Discourages final closure	Requires conclusive end

(as adapted from Peter Winchell)

1. Understanding vs. Proving the Other Side Wrong

The first "Habit of Mind" which must be altered for a successful Socratic Dialogue (used here synonymously with "Seminar") is the basic tendency in society to stick to our guns and prove the other side wrong rather than willingly opening our minds to the possibility that other viewpoints may be more valid or more incisive than our own. Since teenagers, in particular, already know everything, they have become all too used to dismissing other opinions. [I'm sure teachers of elementary and intermediate school students can easily substitute those age groups for teenagers here.] Parents, for example, when arguing over a curfew, couldn't possibly be correct despite their experience. Similarly, when teens in the classroom setting have fixed ideas (probably ethnocentric at their bases) about a national problem such as homeland security, no evidence will change their opinions. Parental and societal influences come to the forefront of their minds. The students immediately set out in any discussion with the purpose of proving the other side wrong.

Socratic Dialogue, however, has the goal of having students willingly suspend their belief systems in order to give other opinions a chance. Rather than immediately trying to prove the opposition wrong, students must consider all possibilities. This is not easy. It requires a mental process something like this:

> *"I think I'm right, but what Joe is suggesting does make sense. And if I add his comment to Susan's, then the whole poem takes on a different meaning.... Hmm, I almost like it. My original idea still works for me, but I'll give their ideas a try until I hear what others have to add to theirs and mine."*

2. Listening for Meaning vs. Listening for Flaws

Being from Southern California, we often get into arguments about whether the Los Angeles Dodgers or the Los Angeles Angels (of Anaheim) has the better team. Our debates illustrate what happens when someone listens only for flaws. Suppose that I suggest that the Dodger first baseman is better than the Angels'. As I run through his statistics, my opponent never hears more than my first few words. As soon as he realizes I am going to use statistics, he focuses on his statistical counter-argument. As soon as I begin to rattle off the batting average, home runs, etc., he begins a mental compilation of his first baseman's numbers. As soon as he hears me stop, he begins his own litany, never having heard the details of my argument.

To continue the illustration, in a Socratic Seminar, the Angel supporter would listen attentively to every statistic I offer, with the possibility in mind that I just might be right—that the Dodger first baseman is better than the Angels'. In turn, when he displays his statistics for comparison, I would listen and evaluate with the possibility that evidence shows that he is, in fact, correct. The essential difference, then, is that neither side attempts to find only flaws; instead, all the evidence is put on the table for both "sides" to analyze and evaluate.

3. Beginning with an Open-Mind vs. Prejudgment

In order to listen for meaning as suggested above, one must begin with an open mind rather than entering the conversation with a closed mind. Again, our natural state is to allow our egocentric and ethnocentric biases to control our thinking. At our school we run a monthly parent Socratic Seminar. At a recent meeting, our text was an editorial from the *Los Angeles Times* which suggested that it was time that Americans stopped their flag waving long enough to listen to what the rest of the world had to say about our "jingoistic" position in the world. On one side of the circle sat a very high ranking officer from the U.S. Marine Corps. Directly across from him sat a man who began the conversation by saying, "So far, all we've accomplished in the Mid-East is to reduce big rocks to little rocks."

Luckily, both parents brought an open mind (despite the tone of that first comment) to the seminar. As gentlemen, both listened to the other's position, and to other parents who also participated. Neither allowed, at least openly, his own prejudgments to block the possibility that the other had something valuable to say. Let it suffice to say, at least from my observation, that both men learned significant lessons that night: the marine found that civilians' points of view should be taken into account when making decisions which affect the whole nation, and the civilian discovered that the dedicated men and women of the armed services truly do believe in what they are doing and do not act without that motivation.

Because volatile subjects often make for the best Seminars, being truly open-minded in a dialogue is not easy. Most of us have pre-set opinions on such subjects as cloning, abortion, gay rights, capital punishment, etc. But again, this is the value of the Seminar. As will be discussed in Chapter 12, students are not "Critically Thinking" unless they are able to see at least two sides of every issue. Thus, the essence of Critical Thinking becomes the foundation of the Socratic Seminar.

4. Looking for Strength vs. Looking for Weakness

Part of this same syndrome of being convinced that we are always right is that some built-in need for power or dominance appears to permeate our subconscious. To that end, we seem to have a propensity for assuring our own strength and, at the same time, searching for weaknesses in even our best of friends. I am somewhat fascinated by "couples" in my class who go out of their way to prove each other wrong. Strangely, married couples at the beginning of the parent Socratic Seminars seem to want to do the same thing. This "habit of mind" must be broken for students to open their minds and to attempt to find new meanings.

A good start in this endeavor is to have students, at least at the beginning, purposely look for strength in someone else's statement and look for weakness in their own. Early this school year, my class conducted a Seminar on a reading about whether or not "Black English" was really a language. In order to drive home the habit of looking for strength in someone else's point of view, I stopped the Seminar without warning and had the students write down the strengths of others' statements with which they did not agree. Then I asked them to write down potential holes in their own comments. When forced to do this, the students were astonished to find that, on paper, some of their peers' opinions were more logical or valid than their own. One student in particular, who had voiced the opinion that Black English was not a language, not only found himself agreeing with his "opposition," but was actually able to establish a criteria for what constitutes a language based on others' comments. I find this a useful exercise in the early stages of Seminar training.

Since stopping a Seminar in mid-stream is not really a good idea because the class seldom can recover its intensity, the teacher may want to employ a different tactic to accomplish the same goal. One such method is to include a question on the General Evaluation (see Chapter 6) such as *"What statement with which you did not originally agree made the strongest or most conclusive argument?"* This method may not be quite as effective as stopping the Seminar, but the flow of the Seminar is preserved.

5. Not Requiring Closure vs. Arriving at a Definitive End

There are two great evils taught by master teachers everywhere. The first is that young teachers shouldn't smile for six months. Goodness knows that in the modern world, kids, whether they are ten or fifty, need all the happiness they can get. The second evil is even more important: closure is needed at the end of every lesson. I cannot tell you how many times I have witnessed the following scenario. An English teacher has a fabulous discussion of a poem. The students have been insightful and engaged for forty minutes. They have owned the lesson. Then the teacher notices only five minutes remain before the bell. He halts the discussion and announces,

> *"That was truly a great discussion. You had some really super observations. Now, because we have only five minutes left, I'm going to tell you what Robert Frost really meant in his poem."*

This demand for closure knows no limits by subject matter or grade level. Even math teachers who manage to escape the formulaic, didactic approach by letting students find their own solutions to problems have been known to state,

> *"Wow, your suggestions were wonderful. I think you showed real innovations with your solutions. But now, because we only have five minutes left, I'm going to show the proper way to work the problem."*

In both these scenarios, two things immediately happen: 1) the students lose ownership of their learning; 2) the students dismiss their own thought processes as inconsequential since they now realize that the teacher will expect *his/her* answer on Friday's test. Long-term learning is killed.

The Socratic Seminar, on the other hand, discourages that demand for closure. Rather, it suggests that there are no absolute answers. If a student can provide good evidence that a particular line from a Frost poem can be interpreted a particular way, and it does not contradict the overall direction of the poem, then the interpretation deserves attention. [As the author of two novels myself, I can attest that students find "nifty" meanings that I didn't realize when I originally wrote the work.] If a student can come up with the correct math answer by traveling a road less taken, then that path deserves attention. [It should be noted that International Baccalaureate examiners, from what is arguably the most respected national or international examination system, reward the student as much on the method of solving a problem as they do for arriving at the correct answer.]

Lack of closure may be, for the teacher, the single most difficult aspect of teaching the Socratic Seminar. We are trained to want closure, to want a definite answer that we can easily score as right or wrong. It is no secret that national movements, such as "No Child Left Behind," are more interested in memorized answers than in long-term memory. The entire American education system is designed so that students spend a particular block of time on each subject with no real world inter-relatedness; we are controlled by our "lesson plans." If we accomplish those pre-set goals or objectives, it has been a good day. In direct contrast, the teacher within the Socratic Seminar system must now learn to let the students leave the room—THINKING, ANALYZING, EVALUATING AS THEY GO !

I love ruining students' lunches. By that I mean I love it when students come back the next day and tell me they discussed our Seminar topic during lunch. They have been at McDonald's discussing whether "people who speak different languages live in different worlds," or "if we can have an idea if we don't have words for it." Interestingly, the parents who attend our Seminars are the very worst at this. Because their jobs are rewarded by cars sold, tasks completed, or cases won, closure is second nature. We have yet to conduct a parent seminar where at least one parent doesn't say, *"Wait! We can't leave yet. We don't know the answer."* I just tell them to do as their sons and daughters do—*go home and think about it*.

CHAPTER 3

Three Simple Rules

Although a variety of rules are suggested by the experts, only three are essential for teachers of well-run classrooms. Perhaps many other rules are contained within these three, but these are the students' "Commandments."

1. Listen!
You may not start a sentence until the previous speaker has finished.

The art of listening is indeed a lost art. Blame it on anything you want: talk radio with its multiple hosts trying to out-talk multiple callers; the constant need for noise, whether it be music or TV; the belief that we are always right and everyone else needs to listen to us; the modeling of TV sitcom role models with their constant blather. Who knows for sure? But we have stopped listening.

Evidence of this is clear when we see three students in a group who are all talking at the same time or when we are bothered by cell phone users in the airport who never stop talking, and therefore cannot possibly be listening. Society's listening habits remind me of my childhood when my family would go on long road trips (before there were TV screens in every car). For entertainment we used to sing "Row, Row, Row Your Boat," with each member of the family starting one line behind the previous singer. Thus, all five of us would be singing at the same time, but always one line off. It was impossible to focus on what the others were singing. Modern conversations seem to be headed that way. Simply, we can not talk and listen at the same time.

Since the concept behind the Socratic Seminar is the understanding and evaluation of others' thoughts and opinions, it is obviously essential that we hear what the previous speakers have said. Continuing the flow depends directly on building on, not ignoring, others' comments. If we are not listening because we are thinking only of what we want to say, the dialogue is easily stymied, and the seminar becomes, instead, a series of monologues.

One danger about which the beginning Seminar practitioner should be forewarned is that students, when the Seminar is first brought to the classroom, may want to make one very "wise" comment to impress others and score participation points with the teacher. This causes the student to focus more on how to work in the comment than on being a contributing part of the conversation. Again, the student tunes out what others are saying. Simply discussing this bad habit ahead of time seems to work well. Perhaps the teacher can suggest that more "participation points" are scored by insights which build on another's statement than by one that is "out there," even if by itself the "out there" thought is excellent.

No matter what the grade level, teachers may wish to employ artificial means of controlling the listening during the first few sessions. *The teacher does not want to call on students with raised hands* because that puts the teacher in the position of teacher rather than as an equal participant with the students. From my observations, these methods work best:

a) **the Conch** — Everyone remembers that in Lord of the Flies the boy who held the conch had the right to speak until he passed the shell to someone else, who then had the power. Any symbolic "conch" will work in the Seminar, but many practitioners actually use a real one. One of my greatest achievements as a teacher came when a deaf student checked into our school and he spoke for the first time in his high school career because of the Socratic Seminar. We were connected through a wireless "bean" (a "microphone" attached to my shirt) and his earpiece. I decided to use the bean in place of a conch; thus the person who held the bean had the right to speak. When the deaf student held the bean, he knew others would listen closely (despite his severe speech problem). He soon gained confidence and by the end of the semester would lend two or three really good comments in every Seminar.

b) **Cards** — Some teachers give each student three cards (or flags) and after speaking, the student must toss the card into the middle of the circle. Thus the student is limited in what he/she can say. Most often then, the student will not mindlessly interrupt others, but rather, wait patiently for the proper time to add to the dialogue.

c) **Students Calling on Students** — A very simple method of controlling the tendency not to listen to fellow students is to have the speaker call on the next speaker. Probably the most efficiency will come when potential speakers raise their hands. Proper etiquette also forces the potential speakers to keep their hands down until the speaker finishes. Subtle hand gestures rather than waving and squirming also help. Thus the Seminar promotes civility and discourages rudeness.

The beginning teacher should not worry that these methods will need to be employed for too long. Students whom I have observed, whether they be kindergartners or college students, quickly learn to be cordial listeners. If anything, the teacher may get wary of students who accidentally begin simultaneously engaging in a conversation and then proceed with *"Oh, I'm sorry, go ahead."* ... *"No, that's ok, you go."* ... *"No, you ...."* However, over-politeness these days can not be construed as a bad thing.

2. Refer directly to the text.

One of the things which make the Socratic Seminar methodology so valuable is the need for students to delve into the "text" (the reading, picture, problem, etc. used as a basis for the dialogue—see Chapter 11) far more deeply than what they usually do. Modern students (and this habit only seems to get worse as the students get older) are prone to do things as quickly as is humanly possible, regardless of the quality of the work. That means that they can explicate a poem by T.S. Eliot in five minutes and be perfectly happy with their analysis. They can take one look at a "Persistence of Memory" by Salvador Dali and think they have garnered from it all the hidden meanings Dali intended with "those stupid soft watches."

In sharp contrast, the Seminar requires that the students take the poem apart word by word, line by line. It demands that students diagnose every nuance of a painting and explore every possible meaning. Students learn to search for subtleties rather than to arrive quickly at generalizations. It forces students to wonder why a poet such as Stephen Crane uses "mumbles" instead of "says" in "The Wayfarer." It coerces the viewer to reexamine the apostle sitting next to Christ in DaVinci's "Last Supper" as a basis for evaluating modern theories about his/her identity.

To this end, three things are essential:

a) All written texts must be numbered down the side, and students must always refer directly to the line by number. *"I question what Hitler meant in line 23, when he said .... "* Or *"Frost could mean two things in line 15 when he says... "* The same holds true with a reading from a science journal or an article on mathematical statistics.

b) The teacher must constantly model that habit, particularly with the opening question. *"If you notice in line 56 the author refers to the theory of evolution as... Can you explain what...?"*

c) Students must be trained never to stray far from the text. Some asides might be pertinent, and in fact, might allow a neophyte, reluctant speaker into the conversation, but these comments should form a very minor portion of the dialogue. Each teacher must know the class and each individual in it, and therefore, the value of allowing, in one class, what might be considered "stray" comments in another. For example, in a lower-ability class, slightly off-text comments might be more acceptable because those comments might provide the vehicle for relevance and thus total class involvement.

I have witnessed a variety of successful teaching styles and cannot conclude that there should be an exact rule regarding the need for precise rules on the relevancy of student input; however, I can safely conclude that the more "connected" the offerings to the text, the more valuable the entire Seminar is to the understanding of the text. For this reason, both

Advanced Placement and International Baccalaureate teachers love the Seminar methodology. The Seminar provides close analysis at its finest.

3. Build on, rather than tear down, others' comments.

Over the years I have been hired by a variety of groups from school boards to college student body leadership teams to teach the Socratic Seminar as a means of civil conversation between those who previously could not accomplish their goals because the members were in attack mode rather than in a mood to listen, digest, comprehend, and evaluate through meaningful dialogue. We all seem to be convinced that we have the right answers to any problem, and everyone else would do well to listen to us. Few of us ever sit quietly and listen to another's views with the possibility that someone else could have a better answer or solution.

Because we have learned the art of debate and it has become a habit of mind, we are always on the defensive. When someone else begins to speak, we immediately begin to form the counter-argument. Thus we stop listening. Therefore, any attempt at understanding is lost. We hear only flaws in the argument—never the strengths. This seems somewhat natural in modern society.

However, this is just the beginning. I do not think it is imprecise to suggest that modern children, whether they are six or sixteen, are too often disrespectful, if not downright rude to their classmates. Seldom do they actually compliment a classmate with a *"You're right." "That's stupid"* or worse *"That's retarded"* slips from their mouths with ease. Because they are used to being in debate mode at the dinner table, in the classroom, or even on a date, students are not in the least bit reluctant to say, *"You're wrong!"* And because it has become a cliché, *"You're absolutely wrong."* All of these phrases dam up any possible flow of ideas. The students stop trying to understand.

Thus, we must create ways to train students to build on each other's comments rather than tear them down. If we want to disagree, we must do it agreeably. The simplest way is to ask a question rather than make a statement:

> ***Not:*** *"That can't be right. Everyone knows that science and religion..."*
>
> ***But:*** *"Isn't it possible that science and religion can ...?"*
>
> ***Or:*** *"Can you explain to us why science and religion can't...?"*

If we refer to the chapter on the art of questioning (see Chapter 7), we will find that many of those basic questions are not only less abrasive than putting another student down, but also more likely to lead to further understanding:

> ***Not:*** *"You don't know what you're talking about when you say..."*
>
> ***But:*** *"Are you assuming ... when you say...?"*

Or: *"Isn't there some bias involved when you suggest that...?"*

Not: *"I know you're wrong. I just read that..."*

But: *"Is that your opinion or do you have evidence that...?"*

Or: *"Can you give us the source of those statistics...?"*

Not all disagreements, however, lend themselves so readily to questions. Sometimes one student simply disagrees with another and wants to contradict the previous statement. Again, it is important that this is done in a civil manner which shows respect for the other student and his/her opinion. For this reason, many of our freshmen teachers post "helping" phrases on the wall for easy reference by the students:

"That's interesting because I was thinking..."

"I hear what you're saying, but doesn't line five..."

"I'm a bit confused. I thought maybe..."

"I could accept that if only line seven didn't..."

"Can you clarify what you meant by ... because ...?"

"I might be mistaken, but line nine seems to suggest something else."

"I don't think you and I are quite on the same page on this because ..."

"Perhaps we should consider an alternative viewpoint."

Obviously, every teacher needs to compile his/her own list depending on the age or sophistication of the students. The bottom line is simply that we want students to build on each other's comments. Teachers will soon find students even using the word *build* in their comments: *"Just to build on what Josh said..."* Believe it or not, I have actually had students tell me the class is getting *"too nice"* to each other—that it was more fun when they *"tore each other apart."* Fine, let them do that elsewhere; my goal is to have them listen, understand, and grow.

CHAPTER 4

The Basics for Getting Started

To begin, the teacher must visualize a circle of 20, perhaps a maximum of 25 students engaged in an idyllic conversation. After this one sentence, a good percentage of you are ready to throw this book in the trash and announce, *"Great, the future of education and I have 40 students in my class!"* Do not despair. The Seminar does involve 20 – 25 students at one time, but there are at least two methods by which a class of 40 can successfully utilize the methodology. Keeping the Seminar at a maximum of 25 is important because 100% participation is one of the essential values of this methodology.

First, the teacher must be willing to accept one essential element necessary to the success of the Seminar: the teacher and the student become equals. This means no teacher and no student roles. Equals! We all learn! 6'1" male teachers may already see a problem. How do we sit in the same seat in the circle as a first grader? Simple. You do it! Start exercising and stretching. You can do it! More later....

Second, the teacher of 40 students must utilize one of two methods to reduce the circle to a manageable 20 – 25: the "Inner and Outer Circle" technique, or the "Hot Seat" technique.

Inner and Outer Circle

The "Inner and Outer Circles" are by far the most common of the two methods. Just break the class in half—one half in the inner circle, which actually participates in the Seminar, and one half in the outer circle which evaluates the students in the inner circle (see Chapter 6). At some point, the circles are reversed. The inner circle then becomes the outer circle and then evaluates their partners who had previously evaluated them.

In the following diagram, the circle with the diagonal lines represents the teacher (or "facilitator"). The two students with "crosses" (one in the inner circle and one in the outer circle) are partners for peer evaluation. Likewise the two with "circle X's," etc.

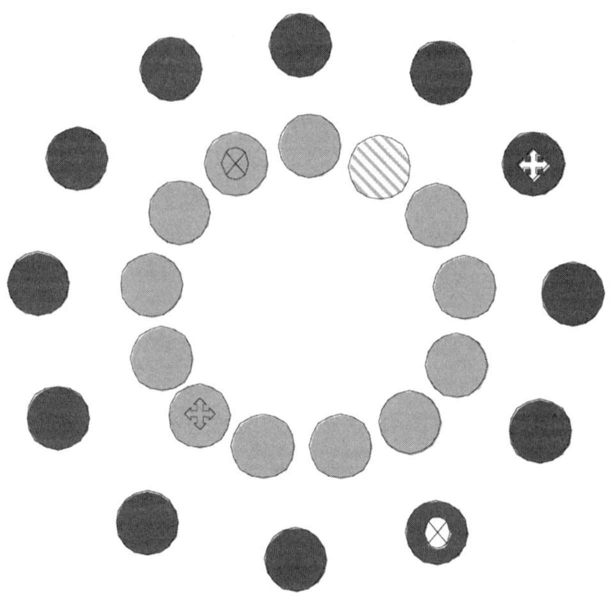

Inner & Outer Circles

Several ways to utilize this break are commonplace. In an English class, the first inner circle might dialogue with one poem and the second a related poem. Or perhaps the two circles might dialogue on two parts of a poem… or two passages from a novel. In social science, a similar activity might take place. I recently divided my class into three groups. The first dialogued on Socrates' "Apology." The second delved into one paragraph from Thoreau's "Civil Disobedience" (men as dirt). The third engaged in one page of Martin Luther King's "Letter from a Birmingham Jail" (unjust laws). All three groups were responsible (on an essay) for all three. We conducted Seminars during the first 25 minutes of three successive days. In an Art class, the two circles might dialogue on two different, but related, pieces. I recently witnessed two circles discuss DaVinci's and Dalí's "Last Supper(s)." Again, in each case, the teacher becomes a part of—an equal—in each of the circles, always careful to say no more than the students, unless it is absolutely necessary.

Hot Seat

The "Hot Seat" method can be used effectively any time the teacher is not needing to give every student in the class equal opportunity to speak. In the following diagram, two empty seats are spaced within the circle. These seats will be used by students not in the original circle who want to jump into the conversation. They will assume a seat, be recognized as soon as possible, and then vacate the seat as soon as they have spoken.

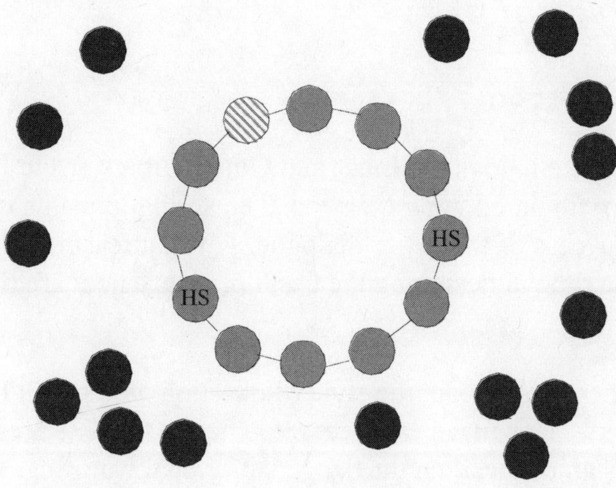

Hot Seats

I often use this method when something is in the morning newspaper that cannot go unnoticed. For example, suppose a high government official makes a speech which makes no immediate sense and needs explanation. Or perhaps it makes all too much sense, but is of earth shattering proportions and I think it is important that my students understand the consequences. In any case, I feel I would be derelict in my duties as a teacher if the issue were not hashed over. In this situation, I might use the Hot Seat, as opposed to the Inner and Outer Circle, because my intention is to remain informal with volunteers participating in a non-graded dialogue.

I recently watched a Spanish teacher use the Hot Seat method after she had received an e-mail from a student in Europe who was insulted by her wish of "good luck." The foreign student took that to mean that the teacher thought she had no real chance for success and only luck could help her out. The following day, the teacher held a Socratic Seminar with hot seats on the Theory of Knowledge question, "Do people who speak different languages live in different worlds?"

The Hot Seat method also works well when the teacher wishes to give students the opportunity for "extra credit" points or "participation" points, perhaps at the end of a grading period. In both of these cases, volunteers can form the original circle to begin the dialogue and others can join in at any time by jumping into a hot seat. All involved students must realize the dynamic of recognizing the hot seat students as soon as possible, and those in the hot seats must realize that because they did not volunteer for the original circle, they forfeit the right to stay in the circle for further questioning and subsequent dialogue.

With these two methods, teachers should be able to cope with the ridiculous class sizes we face daily. No teacher should dismiss the Socratic Seminar strictly because of the numbers.

The Opening Question

Whether the teacher employs the Inner and Outer Circles or the Hot Seat method, the Seminar must begin with an opening question. The strength of this question might determine the degree of success of the entire dialogue. For that reason, it behooves the teacher to spend considerable time in designing the best opening. There are two goals which must be accomplished:

1. The teacher must model the style of question which will be expected from the students. This means a direct reference to the text is essential. Suppose the text is an editorial on the dangers of global warming.

   Not: Do you think we are in immediate danger?

   But: In line 25, the author calls the threat "imminent." What evidence does he offer to support that claim?

   The students are then expected to refer directly to a specific line when answering that question, and hopefully, will continue to refer directly to the text throughout the dialogue.

2. With an extremely animated and vocal group, this may be the teacher's last chance to steer the conversation toward a particular point. Suppose the text is an excerpt from "Picasso at the Lapin Agile," by Steve Martin. Since the purpose of the dialogue might be to show that both the scientist and the artist must use imagination, the teacher may wish to open the dialogue with a "can't miss" question.

   In line 14, the barmaid, Suzzanne, can't dance without music, but both Picasso and Einstein can. Why?

Since the opening question plays such a key role, the teacher would be wise to have three or four questions ready before the dialogue begins. Depending on the sophistication of the group and their ability to carry the Seminar without teacher intervention, the teacher may well need or want to use the other questions later in the dialogue. As facilitator, the teacher must keep the dialogue moving, and therefore, those additional questions are often of value.

One final note. The teacher must not be afraid of silence following the opening question. Let the students think. The silence will be a bit uncomfortable for them, and they will soon jump in. Even a full minute is not too much time. Students get little enough time to think without the teacher answering for them!

CHAPTER 5

Helpful Hints for Beginners

1. Until you and your students feel confident and comfortable, **keep your Seminars short**. 20 to 25 minutes is a good limit.

2. If you are using a written text, **keep the text short**. As tempting as it may be to cover everything you want covered in a particular lesson, this is one case where **less is definitely more**. 20 to 30 lines is a good limit. You definitely do not want to begin your experience with a two page document.

3. **Number the lines of your text**. Remember that you always want students to refer to specific lines: *"If you look at lines two and three, you will notice that Frost says..."*

4. **Prepare 3 or 4 opening questions**. This will allow you to have a last minute choice of questions, and it will allow for some re-direction if the Seminar bogs down because your opening question did not serve the purpose for which you had hoped (see Chapter 4).

5. Be patient. **Don't be afraid of silence**. Often, silence means students are thinking. Remember, the average teacher allows only one second for students to answer a question before he/she answers for the students, but the brain might need at least three seconds to process a question. Students are uncomfortable with silence, and a minute or two will put their brains in overdrive... a good thing.

6. Use both the **Inner and Outer Circle** and the **Hot Seat** methods to control the size of your circle since 100% participation is desired. It should never exceed 25 (see Chapter 4).

7. Although a circle is preferable, a **square** formed by tables will obviously work almost as well if that is the only possibility in a particular classroom.

8. Design your own **evaluation sheets** to fit your classroom needs. Keep them simple, so the evaluator can focus on the text (see Chapter 6).

9. **Control the conversation hog** in one of three ways: a) use a group evaluation sheet and after class mention to the hog that several students made ref-

erence to that student trying to dominate; b) give each student three cards. After a comment, the student tosses in the card, thus limiting each student to three comments; 3) have the "dominator" evaluate the whole group. When made to be the chief evaluator, the dominator will see what he/she is doing.

10. With younger, or less mature, students **repeating the three rules** before the Seminar begins, is always a good idea.

11. If the Seminar **lapses into debate mode**, don't be afraid to stop the Seminar and restate the three key rules. Most often, students will be disappointed in their "failure" to follow the requirements of the dialogue and will quickly return to proper form. Obviously, the teacher should be as subtle or as unobtrusive as possible with this "reprimand."

12. Use **"participation points"** to encourage participation by every student. Don't be afraid to pause with five or so minutes left and say, *"Ok, we have just a few minutes left, and there are just a couple of you who have not yet spoken. Since you all need the participation points, if you have already made a comment, let's let those who haven't have a chance now."* The facilitator may even want to prepare a fresh question for these students. As these reticent students gain confidence, they will be more willing participants in subsequent Seminars.

13. **Heap the praise on reluctant speakers** after class. You might say, *"Wow, Johnny, that comment you made about geometry being more useful than algebra in real life was really interesting. You should put in your two cents more often."* Of course, you do not want to say it front of others because it will come across as phony.

14. **Post helpful lines** for building rather than tearing down (see Chapter 3).

15. **Use good follow-up questions to steer students** toward a point, but never force the issue. You never want to say, *"But you're missing a key point. You have to look at line 12 if ...."* Rather, you might ask, *"After hearing Fred's comment, I'm curious what you think the author meant in line 12 when he...."* In this manner, you don't steal ownership of the lesson away from the students, and you can always emphasize a particular point the next day.

16. **Don't be disappointed** if the dialogue does not go exactly where you hoped. Remember that student ownership of only some of the intended lesson is still more valuable than teacher ownership of a complete lesson. With 20 good minds working together, something valuable will happen.

17. **Don't attempt to continue a Seminar the next day**. It is impossible to return to the same pitch and moment.

18. **Vary your sources**. Using related news articles will keep your class relevant. Using art will provide interdisciplinary thinking. Every subject discipline has its own problems which need solutions.

19. Common sense should dictate the amount of "**Reading Time**" in preparation for the Seminar (see Chapter 11). Very difficult texts might require homework the night before. Simple texts might require only five minutes immediately before the Seminar begins.

20. **Enjoy yourself** and let your students know it. This is your chance to learn from them. Model your pleasure in the learning process.

CHAPTER 6

Evaluation Sheets

The purist might say that the Socratic Seminar is too beautiful, too perfect a methodology to be tainted by the awarding of grades based on performance. It does seem that in the ideal world, students should be able to speak freely some time in their education without a grade hanging over their heads. However, in the modern classroom, that concept may be just that—idyllic.

Not that every Seminar has to be graded. Certainly, there are many times when open conversation is not only good, but healthy. Particularly, when using the "Hot Seat" format (see Chapter 4), to have the class decipher some news article in an unplanned lesson, the absence of grades might encourage a more free-wheeling interchange of ideas. The Seminar becomes a reward in itself, and the students will soon begin demanding more frequent Seminars in the class.

Individual Evaluation

On the other hand, individual evaluation sheets might produce excellent results in terms of the implementation of the three basic rules (see chapter 3) and the general conduct of the Seminar. However, I would suggest that these evaluations remain somewhat informal—without a strict, by the numbers, inclusion in a grade book. These sheets might be most easily adapted to the "Inner and Outer Circle" format. Simply pair the students up—one outer circle student evaluating one inner circle student. The roles reverse when the circles reverse. The evaluator should sit directly opposite the student being evaluated so that body language, including facial expression, can be factored in. In the following diagram, the letters are matched for peer evaluation. The circle with the diagonal lines represents the facilitator.

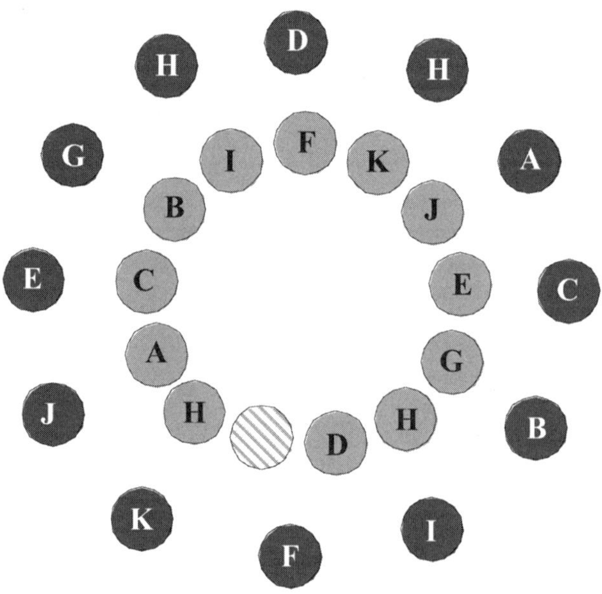

Inner & Outer Circles with Evaluation

The individual evaluation sheets should be created to meet the needs of the individual class based on age, subject discipline, and ability level. For example, I am more interested in the sophistication of the responses in my honors class than in my "workshop" class. When ELL (English Language Learner) students are involved, I want to take note of the courtesy offered by native English speakers as they listen to the ELL students. The following is a basic evaluation sheet that might be used as a jump-off point for other evaluative tools:

A - Excellent

Does not interrupt other speakers ____________

Refers directly to the text ____________

Builds on others' comments ____________

Reflects an open-minded stance on issues ____________

B - Good

At times begins speaking before another is done ____________

Does not always refer to specifics of text ____________

Contradicts, but does so civilly ____________

Appears close-minded in stance on some issues ____________

C - Fair

Interrupts others ____________

Comments relate only marginally ____________

Puts down others' comments ____________

Refuses to consider other viewpoints ____________

Speaks without thinking ____________

Uses too many "ums," "you knows" ____________

D - Unsatisfactory

Attempts to dominate the dialogue ____________

Unprepared with text ____________

Obviously, the difference in levels (A, B, C, D) presents a fine line. And, too, some categories become very subjective, such as "appears ...." My suggestion would be that the evaluation sheet be used mostly as a tool for improvement of the seminar. For example, a student who attempts to dominate, or even who gets carried away and dominates accidentally, needs to know that. The "Unsatisfactory" label certainly addresses that and, if one student can cordially point out that flaw, the next Seminar should run more smoothly. If the sheets are to be used for "real grades," perhaps they are best left as "participation points."

General Evaluation

The general evaluation also serves several valuable functions. First, it is a good way to stop the inevitable "dominator." I would never embarrass a student in front of everyone else, but the general evaluation sheet allows me to pull the student aside, perhaps after class, and mention that *"eight different students pointed out that you tried to dominate."* I would be sure to couch that comment in the positive: *"I really liked what you had to say today about fractals. I find it very interesting. However, eight.... Maybe in the next seminar, you should limit yourself to just two or three comments, and think about exactly how you want to phrase those comments, first. As I said, your insights are great, but we have to make sure everyone has an equal opportunity to talk."*

A second very valuable function comes for the opportunity to compliment the insightful student and the reticent student. Even if no one really mentions the comment of the reticent student, a little white lie might reap huge rewards: *"Joe, a couple people listed you as making a good comment that moved the conversation yesterday. Keep it up. I'd like to hear more from you. That was good stuff."*

A third value might come from the evaluation of the teacher. Being "just" the facilitator is not easy, particularly when we have a pretty good idea that we have the "right answer." Even when we think we have held ourselves in check, sometimes we add an explanation that robs the students of ownership. I also like the students to evaluate my opening question—to see if it was a good conversation starter.

With these values in mind, the following general evaluation sheet could prove useful:

Socratic Seminar General Evaluation

1. What was the best point made during the seminar? By whom?
2. Who helped move the dialogue forward? How?
3. Who lapsed into debate rather than dialogue? About what?
4. Did any student attempt to dominate the discussion?
5. Did the teacher's opening question stimulate worthy conversation?
6. Did the teacher or leader fit in as an equal with the students?

CHAPTER 7

The Art of Asking Questions

Socrates is best known for making students think by asking them questions, rather than filling their short-term memory by lecturing in didactic fashion. Hence, any dialogue which can carry the label "Socratic" must necessarily involve questioning. Since in the Socratic Seminar, all members (students and teacher) are equals, the inquiries must necessarily come from all in attendance. To this end, I begin the year with ten questioning techniques which I think all students of all ages and ability levels should be able to utilize with varied degrees of sophistication.

Before I describe the basic ten, it is important to take note of Bloom's Taxonomy —that hated, but integral, part of every student teacher's life—and realize the Taxonomy also applies directly to the intellectual value of particular kinds of questions:

Fact

Who was the sixteenth president?

Comprehension

Why do a feather and a marble fall at the same rate in a vacuum?

Note: 90% of all teachers' questions come from these two lower level thinking skills!!!! That leaves only 10% for the four higher levels:

Application

Can your life be reduced to mathematical formulas?

Analysis

Do people who speak different languages live in different worlds?

Synthesis

How do the female protagonists in The Great Gatsby and The Sun Also Rises compare?

Evaluation

Is the "prevent defense" a failed concept in high school football?

The ten questioning techniques described below cover the spectrum of Bloom's Taxonomy. All are necessary for clear understanding. However, we should always keep in mind a major goal of using the Seminar dialogue – by listening and questioning to move into the higher levels of critical thinking. To this end, we will now discuss the ten essential questioning methods (originally adapted from Timothy Crusius):

1. Ask if you have understood the speaker's position.

When one member of the circle asks another, "Am I understanding correctly that you are saying that social scientists always misuse statistics to make their point, and therefore we can never trust sociological studies?" two important dynamics take place. First, the original speaker re-thinks his original statement and most likely will alter it to make it more exact. For example, in this case, the speaker will probably retract the words always and never. The original statement was a hasty generalization and the speaker, when asked for clarification, will realize his error. Even if there is not an error in the original, the speaker's second attempt at the same statement will be refined and made clearer.

The second dynamic is that everyone in the circle does, in fact, get clarification. If a subtlety was missed the first time, it should not go unnoticed in the second. When re-stated, each member of the circle has a chance to re-digest the statement and see if he/she can build on that statement. In short, everyone profits from clarification.

2. Ask for definitions of any words that seem central to the position.

Most of us assume that because we speak English, we all mean the same things when we use the same words. However, that is not true. Take a simple word like evil. When I ask teachers in a workshop the meaning of the word, they suggest "the opposite of good," "bad," "purposely hurting another," "subversive," "purposely damaging," "malintentioned," "satanic," "the opposite of God's character," etc. Each of those carries a different connotation and most likely some in the crowd never thought of anything close to a definition such as "the opposite of God's character."

Further illustration comes from the use of *evil* by President George Bush when justifying the Iraq War. He stated he wanted "… to rid the world of *evil* doers." Interestingly, *The American Heritage Dictionary* defines the word as "… causing ruin, injury, or pain… characterized by anger or spite." Without much effort, one could certainly suggest the existence of "evil" on both sides of the war.

Meanings can also be cultural. On one occasion, when demonstrating the Socratic Seminar technique with fifteen inner-city, African-American fifth graders, with the "Pledge of Allegiance," I asked the circle what two words they thought were added in the 1950s that are very controversial. Of course, I expected "under God." A student raised his hand and said, "*For all.*" When I asked why, the fifth grader said, *"Words like* liberty *and* justice *are white man's words. Blacks don't have liberty or justice...."* The fifty observers and I all learned an important lesson that day.

Thus, the meaning of every word in the text is central to the understanding of that text. Very often, then, the teacher might even want to begin by asking if there are any words the definition of which any student finds confusing or nebulous. But often, a student will use a word that needs clarification. Perhaps the word is one with several meanings, i.e. *sacrifice*, or perhaps it is one for which few students actually know the meaning, i.e. *disinterested* (as opposed to uninterested) which means "objective or unbiased." In both of these cases asking for the meaning is essential to understanding.

3. Ask about the assumptions on which the argument is based.

A few years ago, a football recruiter from a very prestigious university asked me to do something which I considered unethical in order to make an excellent, but not very bright, football player eligible to play for that university. When I declined (and chastised him for making the suggestion), he stated, *"Don't you realize you are denying him the possibility for an education at the best university west of the Mississippi River?"* That intrigued me, so I asked why the school was "the best." The coach told me that the school *"had the highest average SAT for incoming freshmen."*

What assumptions was he making? That the SAT relates somehow to intelligence? That the SAT translates into success in school? That the SAT reflects the quality of the university rather than the quality of the high school at which the student earned that score? That a student wants to attend a school where everyone else has a high SAT (I personally would rather compete with people who aren't as smart as I am.)?

Students (and adults) make similar assumptions all the time. If our goal is clarity and understanding, assumptions (which usually involve some type of generalization) should never go unchecked. In the Seminar, students do not have to be "mean" about it; they simply need to word their query as a question: *"Are you assuming that everyone in California is tanned?"* Or just a general question: *"When you referred to the wealth of people in Orange County, what are you assuming?"* The clarification will be critical to continuation of the dialogue.

4. Ask if the statistics used lead to the stated conclusion.

Most of us have heard the anonymous quote, "There are three kinds of lies: lies, damn lies, and statistics." I recently read a newspaper article that stated that a particular university "was a breeding ground for immorality because 8 of 10 students tested for STDs tested positive." At first glance, a student might think, "Wow, 80% of the school has an STD!" However, the student well-trained in the art of Seminar questioning, quickly realizes that the only people tested would be those who went to the clinic because they suspected they might have a disease in the first place.

Indeed, statistics always seem impressive and add a certain air of authority to any statement. It is interesting to listen to the news and watch both the Democrats and the Republicans use exactly the same statistics for both the pro and con arguments on war dead, joblessness, oil prices, etc. They are an easy tool for the wise student—if he/she can get away with it. But well stated questions should always ferret out inaccurate conclusions.

Another common error involving statistics comes from the fallacy called "Ignorantio Elenchi," or arriving at a conclusion which does not follow the premises. This fallacy does not have to, but often involves statistics. For example, a student might state, *"The New York Yankees spend $195 million per year on their players. That is $72 million more than the next highest team, the Boston Red Sox. Therefore, the Yankees have a better team than the Red Sox."* The conclusion may or may not be true, but it is important for students to realize that the conclusion does not come from those statistics. If, for example, the Yankee money was not well spent, or that a high priced ball player was hurt and out for the season, the Yankees would probably not have the best team. Again a simple, well stated question can expose the fallacy.

5. Ask if the conclusions are supported by opinions or evidence.

To understand this line of questioning, one needs only to witness almost any Seminar in the area of science. Common subjects involve DNA research and cloning. It is strange how everyone freely offers expertise on such difficult subjects. [Of course, this expertise is not limited to Socratic Seminars. Lunch table arguments as well as national elections are won and lost because of our vast knowledge here.] However, when I ask an entire audience at a Seminar training who can explain how DNA or cloning works, I might find two teachers out of every fifty who actually think they have a handle on it. And yet we freely offer our expertise at every opportunity. If we take the above 2/50 ratio as valid, that means that only 4% of the statements are based on evidence, while 96% base their arguments on opinion.

As further illustration, I should admit that I have been involved in many Seminars with my students on these subjects. I will gladly offer my belief that we should charge ahead with cloning "body parts." Do I know anything about the science behind cloning (the evidence)? No, not at all. I just know that I need new cartilage in my knee and that I have had several loved ones pass away who could have been saved by cloned organs. Thus my argument is founded entirely on emotion and opinion.

Obviously, the issue of accepting opinion without evidence is not restricted to science seminars. We debate about topics such as illegal immigration, social security, and universal healthcare without a single hard core fact. Students, with their limited experience and limited exposure through reading about these subjects, are often far more guilty than we adults.

6. Ask if the conclusions are logical and consistent.

One of the best examples of this problem is also one of the most painful for many students. This is simply because so many people (including important government officials) are guilty of this inconsistent logic.

Life begins at conception.

Aborting a fetus is killing a life.

Abortion is murder…

…except in the cases of rape or incest.

For the purpose of this illustration, let us not debate the validity of the premises. Rather, we need to focus on the inconsistency of the argument. If we accept that abortion is taking a life, then it is always taking a life. The circumstances under which the female became pregnant are inconsequential. We could just as easily add…except in the case where the girl is under 15…or… except in the case where the father is of a different religion. As ridiculous as this sounds, the statement is just as valid in a purely logical sense.

Another interesting illustration comes from the ongoing debate over "merit pay." The purpose of merit pay could be said to be to improve teaching styles in order to improve student learning. However, logic and history do not dictate this. Rather, if pay is tied directly to student scores on objective tests, teachers will only teach to the test for short-term memory, and little long-term understanding will be gained. The hoped for "conclusion" most likely will not follow.

Again, in the Seminar, we want students to be logical and consistent. Even without formal training in fallacious thinking, students, when given the time and habit of clear thinking should be able to catch similar inconsistencies.

7. Ask if the analogies are fallacious.

Students love analogies! We often hear them say, "That's like ..." or "... "If you say that you might as well say...." Some experts guess that at least 75% of all analogies are based on a faulty comparison.

The classic bad analogy comes from the Vietnam era. *"If you're old enough to fight, you're old enough to vote."* Although many may feel that anyone who puts his/her life on the line in a war should have a right to vote on who is making the decisions, or that same soldier has earned the right to vote on how the government spends taxes, the analogy at its base is still faulty. To be a good comparison, the same skills would be required for both. Again, some would debate this, but arguably the opposite skills are required. We might define the perfect soldier as one who faithfully obeys orders and never stops in mid-mission and says, *"Wait, maybe we should approach from the back side instead. You guys go on ahead without us."* On the other hand, the perfect voter is one who says, *"Wait, I don't know enough about this issue. I need to do some more research on it before I can cast my vote."*

As soon as the critical thinker hears the word *like*, the antenna should go up. In an ethics unit, we recently dialogued with a reading from Dr. Kevorkian, aka Dr. Death, in which he compares our changing attitude toward coal (no longer needed to heat homes) to our changing attitude toward euthanasia (now possibly needed as lives are lengthened by medical advances). The students quickly asked whether life could be compared to coal (Klemke). As suggested above, experts agree that most analogies are just as faulty.

8. Ask about the speaker's bias.

The term *bias* is often misunderstood as necessarily a bad thing—such as in "prejudice." However, bias may also be a positive force. A die-hard Los Angeles Lakers fan is *biased* toward the Lakers. He/She might wear a Lakers jersey, watch all their games, etc. In most cases, this is not a negative force.

I am constantly on my students' cases about downloading music illegally or pirating movies from the internet. I tell them in no uncertain terms that judgment day is coming and the gods will punish them for their theft. To understand my harsh stance on this matter, one needs to understand my bias. I am not a musician or a film maker. But I am a writer and copyright laws are very important to me. Hence, I have little use for those who steal another's income by violating those copyright laws. [Or should I compare it to cheating in school just to create another bad analogy?] Students would be a little taken aback by my attitude unless they understood my bias.

Very often, bias is directly tied with values—or what is important to an individual. As illustration, several years ago my students corresponded on a weekly basis with students from Eureka High School in the logging country of Northern California. This was at the time when "Julia Butterfly" was protesting the logging by sitting in a tree for more than a year, and the students were blocking the cutters by surrounding trees and holding hands. Knowing little about the area, my students could not understand the mixed messages they were receiving. While some students were standing their ground against the police who were spraying them with pepper spray, others were writing to us about what horrible people these students were. They painted them as evil and demonic. But we did not understand their biases. Eureka is, in fact, composed of two completely separate groups: the "tree huggers" and the loggers and their families. In other words, while half the students were trying to protect the trees, half of our correspondents' families' livelihoods depended on cutting down these same trees. To understand their statements, one must understand their biases.

No one is free from bias. We all have our values and the accompanying opinions. As conversation progresses around the Socratic circle, students must be careful to decipher the bias of the writer of the text, but also the bias of each individual speaker. Again, the point is to further the understanding, not to "call out" a fellow student. It should be done civilly: *"Joe, do you think that your religious views might be influential in your stand on overpopulation in third world countries?"* No one is hurt by this question, but an essential point of realization might soon be made.

9. Ask about implications.

This line of questioning is most important when the Seminar is used for solving problems. For example, our faculty solves many problems using the Socratic Seminar because it calls for a civil and cordial relationship between the participants on points that will obviously find great disagreement. In similar fashion, in classes such as History or Science, solutions are often sought to solve the world's ills.

Unfortunately, few seem to think of the future consequences of here and now actions. Whether we are speaking of government leaders deciding on issues which might cause a loss of lives or of a teen making a decision which might create a life, we just seem to have a problem seeing beyond a day or a week. Perhaps we would all be wise to follow the "Seven Generation" rule of the Native Americans: no decision should be made until we know the consequences for seven generations hence.

Let us now look more closely at this question's use in the Socratic Seminar. Suppose a ninth grade cultural geography class is discussing a difficult issue, such as AIDS in Africa. The students are likely to come up with interesting solutions, but they may or may not be workable in the long-term. If we suggest a couple should be tested before the first date, will that have emotional consequences down the line? If we promote male circumcision, will that have cultural or religious ramifications? If we send U.S. watchdogs to "enforce" training programs, will we end up with an obligation that still exists 50 years from now? If a student in the circle suggests we develop Africa into a sports mecca to give youth something to do other than sex, are we then imposing our own ethnocentric values and attempting to change African cultural forever, against their will?

The same care for future consequences should be applied at every grade level. Third graders might be studying different kinds of pollution: water, air, noise, etc. To combat smog, a child might naively suggest getting rid of trucks or maybe even getting rid of just diesel trucks. A teacher's guidance would likely be necessary to get students to see the consequences – huge leaps in consumer costs for everything from produce to automobiles. We can never start too young in the effort to have people think ahead to the consequences of their actions.

10. Ask whether the speaker takes opposing views into account.

The essence of critical thinking is the practice of seeing things from more than one point of view, analyzing the two viewpoints, and then evaluating them. This is an essential element of student maturation as ethnocentric and egocentric biases are put to the side in an effort to find objectivity. As much as this remains a goal of the overall Seminar, it is also a necessity for individual participants in the progress of the dialogue. Even when something seems obvious, another possibility exists. Suppose a couple happens upon a car that has its front bumper embedded a few inches into the soft back bumper of the car parked in front of it. Certainly one will remark, *"Oh my gosh, that person didn't even realize he ran into the back of that car. He's messed up when that other guy comes out and sees his car's been hit."* However, the astute partner might then suggest, *"Maybe not. Maybe the front guy backed into the other car when he was parallel parking in that tight space and just didn't realize it."* We should never limit ourselves to only one possibility.

This anecdote just serves to illustrate that opposing views exist for every answer. One student may be "absolutely" sure that illegal immigrants should not hold drivers' licenses because that would be rewarding a "criminal," but a strong counter-argument exists that if we allow illegals in the U.S., at least we should make sure that they know how to drive. One student may be "absolutely" sure that Social Security should be privatized so individuals can increase their income in later years, but a strong counter-argument exists that if money is withdrawn now for investment, then the government would not have the money necessary to fund those currently on Social Security.

At the same time, alternate solutions exist for any grade level discussion. Perhaps a second grade teacher stops reading a short story halfway through and asks how the main character might solve his dilemma. From a circle of twenty, at least ten possible solutions can be offered and each of those can be further refined. This is the essence of the Seminar: searching for understanding by listening to alternatives and objectively analyzing all possibilities.

Times have changed. Questions play an ever increasing role in the modern classroom. In the old days, parents used to ask a child when he/she came home, *"Did you learn anything today?"* In the modern home, the parent might ask, *"Did you ask any good questions today?"*

CHAPTER 8

Sample Socratic Seminar A

Grade 11

U.S. Government (Honors)

Text: The text used was a picture from a LIFE Magazine (1998) which shows a protester at the funeral of Matthew Shepard, a Wyoming student who was beaten and killed for being gay. A small text accompanies the picture. The protestor, wearing camouflage fatigues, holds a sign which states, "Freedom of choice is the right to hate." (Note: The only changes in the following dialogue transcript were the removal of colloquialisms which would not be understood by all readers.)

FREEDOM OF CHOICE IS THE RIGHT TO HATE

Teacher: Are there specific things we ought to notice about the man to help us understand his viewpoint even before we look at the sign?

Sabeer: It seems as if he is a member of the army or the marines because he's wearing camouflage, so I was just wondering if that would have any effect on how biased he might be.

Helen: He's a veteran, maybe WWII or Vietnam.

Ryan: He's probably fought for the country. This could mean that he feels he has the right to say whatever he wants. He feels it's his right.

Nathan: Going more in depth with that, I see the word Okinawa on his hat which was in the Pacific Theater, the place of many atrocities in WWII. Japanese soldiers cut off American GI's genitals and beheaded them. They subjected GIs to many cruel and inhumane things. He saw fellow GIs die for citizens' freedom. He has a good reason to be biased.

Chris: Are you assuming all soldiers witnessed the atrocities?

Nathan: Even if he didn't, he still would have to know about them. And he still defended his country.

Lindsay: Following what Nathan said, the war that he was in and his age, 74 (in the short text), adds to his beliefs. His ideas and biases are from the time he grew up. His views on gay rights are probably 70 years-old. According to my grandmother, being gay back then was not only taboo, but forbidden even to talk about.

Prianka: He does look pretty old, but why do you assume the sign has something to do with gay rights?

Alex: Look at the small text. This guy is protesting at Matthew Shepard's funeral.

Prianka: Sorry, my mistake.

Kristen: I agree about the influence of his age, but I want to go back to what Sabeer and Nathan said. I wonder if it makes a difference whether the war was Vietnam, Iraq, or World War II. Why are you making a big deal out of WWII?

Shashank: I think it does make a difference. WWII was a defensive war, and Vietnam and Iraq are offensive wars—not so popular. As a defender of the country, he has more right to protest.

Jacob: Aren't you generalizing about attitudes about Vietnam and Iraq?

Shashank: Maybe. But, and I realize this is another generalization without hard evidence, I think someone 74 might see it that way. We do all look at WWI and WWII vets as heroes. In people's eyes, they've earned some special rights—if they're still alive. Sadly, Vietnam vets don't seem to have that same distinction.

Kevin: I'd love to hear you guys go at it on that topic, but to go back to the text, I think it's also important to note that before the 90s, homosexuals in the military were definitely forbidden, and perhaps his attitude is a direct reflection of his military background more than the particular war.

Jacob: Thanks. I agree.

Ryan: Only recently have gays been accepted in the military at all with the "Don't ask, don't tell" policy. Maybe he feels that if they didn't serve in the military, they haven't been through what he's been through, and maybe that translates into them not fulfilling their obligation as citizens.

Kristen: I also notice that there is a fence there. I was wondering if they expected this to happen during this funeral.

Teacher: (with a smile) You're all Californians. Can someone explain the fence?

Michael: (the only one who knows) I believe that the fence is there to serve as a barrier for the snow that builds up in the wintertime. (In fact, it is just a snow fence.)

Prianka: Regardless of the military experience, I don't think that being old is an excuse for hating someone. I don't think we should make any concessions to anyone because they come from a different generation. Part of life is adapting to changes, and I don't think that hate is acceptable just because someone is old. I understand that they come from another time, but at the same time it's hate and it's not like music where people's tastes don't hurt anyone. It's just not acceptable for them not to grow with the times.

Rayad: I think that his age does make a difference and creates a bias. People tend to grow more conservative as they grow older and chances are that this person has children, grandchildren and even great-grandchildren. Thus age would really color his view.

Lauren: I don't disagree with you in this case, but I would like you to define "conservative." I'm hung up on equating "conservative" and "hate."

Rayad: Point well taken. I really didn't mean to equate the two. I just meant conservative in relation to accepting or not accepting gay rights. I definitely am not saying anyone has a right to hate.

Madison: I agree. And I think his age or upbringing contributes to his hatred because he doesn't understand it, and it is a mystery to him. Oftentimes people hate what they cannot understand because they just don't know enough about it to have knowledge and understand why and how it works.

Jaci: To add to that, he has a little smirk on his face and a thumbs up, I think he enjoys being from the older generation. Could we agree that as people grow older, they're less prone to change?

Kristen: I don't think we can be 100% sure of that, but about the thumbs up, it might not be thumbs up. It just might be harder to move your hand when you have a glove or a mitten on.

Chris: It could be that he is pointing toward the sign or that he is making some type of hand gesture that we can't interpret for sure with or without his glove.

Nathan: Thumbs up is also a military sign for A-Ok. He seems to be approving of his own stance.

Jill: Or maybe of the murder?

Helen: He could be like an umpire signaling "you're out" to the photographer. Ahmed: Or to the people at the funeral.

Madison: Maybe he is just mugging—kind of like we do when someone is taking our picture.

Teacher: Interesting possibilities. Now that we have studied the surroundings, we should move to the sign itself. Before we do, are there any short, last second observations anyone wants to make?

Lauren: I want to point out something nobody has yet. He's from a population of only six people in his town. We seem to be full of generalizations, but my guess is that if we put all this together, we can pretty easily explain his attitude.

Christian: I just want to comment on his dress code in general. I see he's wearing boots and an army hat. I think he's trying to justify that he is American, and if you don't agree with him, you're un-American.

Michael: I must be un-American then. I was just thinking how foreign this guy's thinking is to me. I'm guessing that's why we have red and blue states.

Helen: I hope as we move to the sign we will discuss who's doing the hating. Personally, I think we are wrong to assume that the sign refers to his right to hate. Suppose he is talking about the murderer's right to hate?

Teacher: Yes, I definitely think we need to get to that possibility. Anyone else? Ok. Let's take a look at the sign itself. My first question would be, does the Constitution of the United States guarantee a choice to hate another person?

Lindsey: I'm not sure who first said this statement but a famous quote is "I may not agree with you, but I will defend to the death your right to disagree." While hate is not the best emotion to portray, it still is an emotion. It's like a chemical imbalance and for some people it's easier to control. Some people feel more passionately than others about certain issues. It's still there and it should be allowed to be expressed, but it would be better if it was controlled.

Lauren: The quote is supposedly from Voltaire, who you all know is French, but I don't think anyone knows for sure.

Sabeer: I don't think that the American government can control what you think because that would be oppressive. However, there is a way to control how feelings are manifested in actions. For example, I think you do have the right to hate, but I think that it is inappropriate to display that hate in a negative way. But if you can control it and display it in an appropriate way, like Lindsay said, I think that is all right because you can't control your mind.

Jaci: Please clarify. Are you suggesting having this sign at the guy's funeral, while the family is grieving, is acceptable?

Jamie: Absolutely not. It is disgusting and despicable. I think it is unethical. I'm just answering the original question. We have a right to our emotions. But we have to control them. This should never have happened.

Jill: This, as in the murder, or this, as in the man at the funeral?

Jamie: I meant the man, but both are unconscionable.

Ryan: The government should ensure all of your rights and opinions, but if they hurt other people, they are wrong and unjustified. So under the Constitution and the freedom of speech, he does have the right to hate another person. However, his rights and freedoms are void if he purposefully violates another's rights.

Kevin: As we have studied, there have been cases involving First Amendment rights. I think it's kind of interesting to relate it to that case where the courts overturned Texas's attempt at making it a crime to burn the flag. I wonder what this guy would say about that?

Michael: Allowing any hate, whether it be for the flag or for gays, only leads to violence and that is what tears apart mankind and degrades our society. Don't forget that it was hatred that caused the murder of an innocent gay student in the first place.

Helen: Hence my question a couple minutes ago about the words on the sign.

Kristen: Common sense also has to enter in. I don't care how much you hate someone, or how many pages of the Constitution guarantee the right to have feelings, you just can't do this at the funeral. Doesn't the family have a right to bury their son in peace?

Ahmed: As much as I don't want to take away the protestor's rights, I can't disagree with you. Couldn't he take his sign a few blocks away—out of the sight of the family?

Prianka: Maybe. But he does have a guaranteed right, and he obviously wants his voice heard. If we were all governed by common sense, we wouldn't need the Constitution in the first place.

Chris: Dream on. Supposedly intelligent college students crucified Matthew Shepard for no reason other than that they did not agree with his lifestyle, which, by the way, hurt no one.

Lindsey: I'm going to take the liberty of changing the focus a bit, because I'm really getting mad at this man and I know that probably isn't our purpose. I want to know about the sign itself. Do you think he wrote "Freedom of Choice" to play off his belief, if it is his belief, that being gay is a choice?

Sabeer: Yes, and as much as I hate to give this guy props, the sign borders on being clever—maybe too clever for him.

Jill: Only if people think being gay is a choice. Personally...Oh let's not go there.

Teacher: Good idea. Let's not go there. People will be debating that for a long time. Let's stick to rights and government guarantees.

Nathan: OK. I want to ask if anyone thinks this action alone violates Matthew Shepherd's life?

Ahmed: Yes. Almost as much as the original murder.

Sabeer: Although I want to agree, I also realize the government can't go around locking people up for life for carrying a sign.

Ryan: If we take Sabeer's comment to the extreme, if we prohibit this protest, aren't we giving the government the right to decide what emotions deserve punishment and which don't. I know this would never happen, but couldn't some futuristic, 1984-type, government outlaw jealousy or love.

We could all agree both are destructive in some way. Hate is just one of the natural human emotions that everyone has experienced at some time.

Rayad: Some of you are experiencing hate right now. Admit it, you hate this guy for disturbing this funeral and being proud of it. He sickens most of you! What I'm wondering is what happens to those people who hate the people who hate? Do they get caught in some type of double bind? Are they not allowed to hate because it goes against their own philosophy? But when I start thinking about it that way, it seems that people should be allowed to hate as long as they don't act.

Alex: Building on what Rayad said about the double bind of hating, just because you don't agree with the people who hate doesn't mean that you hate the people who hate. [Smiles all around. The students are obviously amused with their thinking.] Chris: So it's kind of different in that some people are better able to control their emotions. And besides, I've been thinking that the word hate is strong for what I feel about this man. Maybe we don't hate the people that hate, but we feel antipathy toward them.

Kevin: How about nausea?

Shashank: Chris and Kevin, if you were there and saw this man, would you do anything or say anything? We all know the sayings about the danger of doing nothing.

Jamie: Maybe just talking about it is doing something. I don't think any of us are going to forget that sign or the name Matthew Shepard any time soon.

Ahmed: I know I won't!

Teacher: Then perhaps this is a good place to end. I think Jamie's last comment pretty much sums it all up. Thanks for a terrific seminar! We don't have time now, but we'll do a short writing on this tomorrow.

Points worthy of note:

1. The students themselves took the conversation back directly to the text at least twice. The teacher did not have to play the role of teacher.

2. As tempting as it might have been for the government teacher, he never forced the issue of specific related court cases. He let the students retain ownership.

3. The Seminar did contain some disagreements, but all remained polite and civil.

4. The Seminar gave the students an opportunity to apply the First Amendment to something real.

5. The students demonstrated sophisticated questioning. They identified other students' generalizations and assumptions and several times asked for clarifications.

6. All 21 students spoke. Four students spoke four times each.

7. The teacher spoke a total of six times, including the opening question and the last comment, suggesting a follow-up writing assignment.

8. The teacher allowed the Seminar to remain open-ended. There was no real closure. Students were allowed to leave the class continuing to think about the text. They were observed continuing to comment on the picture. [Note: The teacher did have the students complete a follow-up writing assignment the next day: "If you had an opportunity to talk to this man later, what would you say to him?"]

Sample Socratic Seminar B

Grade 3

Science

Text: A human skeleton taken from a high school biology class. The teacher's goal was to have the students look as closely as possible at the bone structure of the human body.

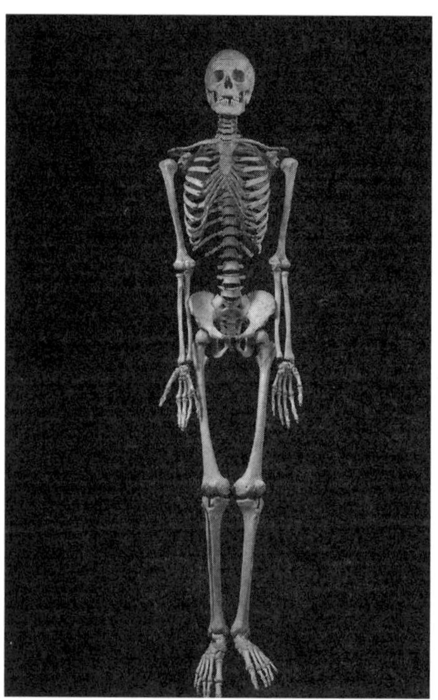

Teacher: My first question is, looking at this skeleton in front of us, what do you think is more important, the skull, because it protects the brain, or the rib cage, because it protects the heart? [Teacher points to both.]

Caitlin: I think it's important to protect the heart because that is how you love. The brain looks like spaghetti anyways.

Arshad: I think they're both really important because my mom always tells me to wear a helmet whenever I go ride my skateboard down the hill. But when she takes me to the doctor, he always checks my heart before everything else. So that's why I think it must be something important.

Nina: I think that the ribs are more important because the chest protects the heart. On a TV show I saw a person in a coma and that means that his brain doesn't work, but he is still alive.

Alex: I think that the rib cage is more important because I learned at Sunday School that Jesus lives inside my heart. He lives inside there and if that broke, he would probably die or get hurt.

Leana: I think that protecting the skull is more important because even if you were still alive in a coma, if you can't think, how can you know if Jesus is living in your heart?

Philip: But I think that the heart is more important because when I give my friend a valentine it's a heart. If your heart goes bad, then you can't have Valentine's Day.

Caitlin: And I think the heart is more important because the rib cage is bigger than the skull so the heart is more important because it needs more protection.

Nina: But I think Phillip was right. Without a brain, you can't know anything anyway.

Stephanie: I don't think Caitlin's right because the heart is not completely closed by the rib cage, but the skull completely goes over the brain so I'm thinking that the brain is more important.

Scott: Well, I know that the heart pumps blood throughout your body and I know that without having a heart, blood can't get to the rest of the body, including the brain.

Lisa: Stephanie was talking about how the skull is on top of the brain, but see how there are lots of ribs around the heart. It's obviously harder to make the ribs in the chest than the skull.

Chris: I think the head is more important because my friend hit his head on a swing and had to go to the hospital. I don't have any friends who had to go to the hospital to fix their hearts.

Stephanie: I think my grandpa died with a heart attack.

Caitlin: I think the man down the street did, too.

Allison: When I watch TV all the time and they're giving CPR, they're always pumping the heart to make the guy live.

Teacher: Sounds like we all agree that both the brain and the heart are necessary for someone to live. Could we say that both the skull and the rib cage are equally important? [Everyone nods.] What do you notice about the rest of the body?

Caitlin: Well, I notice how long the legs are.

Arshad: I think the middle, like the hips are important because the legs are on it and I wouldn't want to try to walk without legs. [Students laugh.]

James: I think that the snake looking thing in the back is most important because it looks like it connects the body together.

Teacher: And by snake, you mean the spine and yes, the spine is a very important structure to any skeleton. The skeleton is made up of many bones that support you and help you stand, sit, and move.

Alex: Well I wanted to know if it is a he-skeleton or a she-skeleton because that might be important.

Lisa: Maybe it's a girl because it looks like she has smaller bones and they look more delicate. If you look at her legs and her fingers they look more like they're going to break.

Arshad: I think it's a boy because his hand looks like he's bouncing a basketball or he is playing baseball and he is running from one of the bases.

Alex: I think it's a she-skeleton because my mom always says that "it goes straight to the hips," and the hips on this skeleton are big; bigger than mine.

Teacher: [laughs] This might be a good place to ask if anyone has ever heard a story about two people named Adam and Eve that involves ribs.

Allison: [waving] I know. I know. God took one of Adam's ribs and made a woman named Eve. And they were the first man and woman on Earth.

Teacher: And so …

Phillip: [after a pause] So Adam is missing a rib.

Amanda: We should count the ribs.

[They all try to count. A variety of numbers come out. The teacher then stands next to the skeleton and one by one points to each. The students count together out loud, until they arrive at 24.]

Teacher: Right. This skeleton has 24.

Phillip: Doesn't look like it's missing a rib.

Amanda: So it's a woman.

Nina: But there isn't an extra one either.

Teacher: I really like how you tried to figure that out, but part of our lesson today should be to know that men and women have the same number of ribs – 24.

Allison: So what about Adam?

Teacher: The story of Adam and Eve is very interesting. Tonight you should all ask your parents about it. And maybe you can teach them about everyone having 24 ribs.... [after a short pause] Any other observations?

Stephanie: I never knew the ribs go around the back. I thought they were just in front.

Lisa: No one said they thought the neck was important. If you didn't have one, your head would fall off.

Caitlin: Yeah, my dad always yells at my brother when he doesn't have his seat belt on: "You're going to break your neck, and then you'll be sorry!"

Teacher: Let's hope you all remember to wear seat belts all the time. Anything else?

Nina: Looking at the bones makes me wonder why they don't break more often because where they connect doesn't look like that strong.

Scott: Now I know why my mother makes me drink milk because bones are white, and I think that's where the milk goes, and she says milk makes bones strong, so maybe that's why they don't break so easy.

Alex: My mom always takes vitamins for her bones.

Teacher: You are all right. Milk has lots of vitamin D, and Alex, I bet your mom's pills contain a mineral called calcium. Both make for strong bones and teeth.

James: I think that it's pretty cool that the body can hold all of the weight. But I don't think the body works all of the time because one time my foot broke, and I think it's because my bones were not powerful enough to hold my whole body.

Amanda: I think that it's funny how the feet look so little. We're so big, but our feet are really tiny. I wonder if that is why I trip all of the time?

Lisa: Hey. I think it's a girl because she has littler feet than a boy's.

[Many nod in agreement.]

Chris: Yah, but I think it's weird how, I never really noticed them before because I can't really see them, but there are a lot of different bones, especially in the hands and feet. I didn't realize there were so many bones in my hands.

Teacher: How many bones do you guess are really in a body?

[Lots of guesses from 20 to 100]

Teacher: There are 206 bones in the body. That's a lot of bones. If you haven't broken one yet, like James did, you're pretty lucky.

Philip: I broke my arm when I fell off a pool slide and had a cast for a long time. I always fall on the ground and get hurt.

Teacher: I bet that hurts. Let's talk some about how you think the bones are attached to each other.

Arshad: I just want to know how the bones stick together. I think that because they're white, well, maybe God put us together using glue and that's how the bones don't fall apart.

Philip: I think that the bones stick together because of gravity. My dad said that everything is held down by gravity, so the bones are held together by gravity.

Allison: I think it's our muscles that hold our bones together because one time I fell off the jungle gym and I sprained my arm and ankle, but I didn't break my bones. Maybe the muscles saved my bones from breaking.

Diane: I don't know how the muscle would stick because the bones are really smooth.

Chris: Chicken leg bones are smooth but there is lots of yucky stuff besides meat. Maybe that's muscles.

Leana: I know when I eat chicken I like the drumstick best, so I wonder which parts of us taste good.

Patrick: I think that the belly is the most delicious part of a person because it's really big and that's where all of my food goes.

[Many in the class groan.]

Amanda: When I'm eating chicken, there is the wobbly stuff that reminds me of rubber and I think that might be what holds the bones together because it's right where the bones meet.

Teacher: I believe you're referring to what are called the ligaments and tendons. That's a good observation.

Stephanie: I think that the joints are pretty weak because when my dad was pulling out my loose tooth yesterday he only used a string to pull it out, and my mom always tells me that my teeth are the strongest bones in my body. I don't think they're held together very well because my dad uses a string to pull them out.

Lisa: Are our teeth bones? Do they count?

Teacher: Yes, teeth are bones. Look at this skeleton.

Nina: I think maybe our skin holds all these bones together. If we didn't have skin, everything would just be all over the floor.

Allison: When my cousin broke his leg in a football game, he said a bone stuck out of the skin. It was really bloody. So I think the skin really helps too because it's thick and that it also helps hold the body together.

Teacher: Diane, you've been pretty quiet, but you look like you really want to say something.

Diane: I was thinking about a worm and a snake. They just wiggle. If they don't have bones, how do they protect their heart and brain?

Patrick: [waving] Oh! Oh! My brother has a snake skeleton. It does have bones.

Teacher: You are right, Patrick. Probably it would be best to save the idea of worm bones for another class since we only have the human skeleton for today.

Lisa: I bet worms have really, really small bones so they can wiggle in tiny holes.

Teacher: We'll talk about worms tomorrow, I promise.... Has anybody decided what bone is most important?

[Many yell out their choice simultaneously. One, Phillip, raises his hand.]

Phillip: I've decided I want to be a skeleton next Halloween.

Teacher: [laughs] Cool. Then we can use you for our conversation.

Points worthy of note:

1. The elementary teacher may have to work harder than upper grade teachers to keep students from straying to personal stories, such as when the students begin to tell the stories of their own broken bones. However, because they give ownership, personal stories are not always bad things.

2. Although the teacher seems to have several goals in mind, she allows the students to think, as in the case of male/female rib count.

3. Without being obtrusive, the teacher does slip in some important facts, such as the vitamin D and calcium comment.

4. The teacher uses a gentle method of including Diane near the end of the dialogue time.

5. Although it does not necessarily come out in the verbal text here, it is clear that the students do notice the structure of the whole skeleton.

6. All 17 students in the inner circle participated at least twice. The teacher spoke 16 times (far more than the high school teacher in Sample A), but all were either for clarification or further inquiry. No comment took ownership from the students.

CHAPTER 9

To Critique or not to Critique

When I first learned the Socratic Seminar methodology some twenty years ago, the "Critique" played a major role in the practice. Basically, the Critique is a "coming down" wrap up after the Seminar dialogue has finished. It provides an opportunity for the participants to discuss (note the purposeful change of verbs from dialogue) what has just taken place. There are several advantages to including a Critique in the day's lesson:

1. Key points can be reiterated.
2. Strengths, such as excellence of questioning, can be identified.
3. Weaknesses, such as general comments on individuals dominating, can be identified.
4. Areas which need work, such as references to the text, can be suggested to better the next seminar.
5. The role of the teacher, as equal participant only, can be evaluated.

There are also several drawbacks to the use of Critique:

1. It takes away time from the actual Dialogue. And in the twenty-first century classroom, time is of the essence.
2. If students know the teacher is going to reiterate the key points anyway, they lose ownership of the lesson.
3. If students are openly evaluated, even in a positive fashion, they may feel singled out and thus be reluctant to speak freely in the future.

Point number one of the disadvantages may be the most significant and is certainly worthy of a short discussion. As we all know, time, in the modern world of standardized tests, is essential. With the pressure of covering centuries of European history in preparation for the AP test, the teacher is reluctant to give up lecture time, even if he/she knows the Seminar will serve the students better for long-term memory. Giving up even more time to evaluate the process seems misplaced. The math teacher attempting to push his weaker students through the basics of algebra for the math portion of the state exit exam might be reluctant to give up time letting students attempt to solve problems on their own, let alone giving up time to talk in detail about how the students did. Again, time is of the essence in the modern classroom.

Socratic Seminar purists, including my original mentor, will be extremely upset to hear this, and Mortimer Adler himself will probably roll over in his grave, but from my observation, currently, far more Seminar practitioners do not use a formal Critique than those who do. Many feel the strengths and weakness can be identified on the evaluation sheets. Most feel they cannot give up the added time for a Critique and, if there is time, they would rather it be spent in actual dialogue.

My suggestion is to let the nature of the class itself be your guide. In my top end Humanities Honors classes, I do not normally use the Critique. The conversation is just too rich to interrupt. I want the students to have complete ownership. My dream is to fade into the background. However, with my reluctant learner, "at-risk" class, a Critique is often essential. Sometimes great points were made, but some students were never quite able to glean the subtleties. This also gives me a chance to praise certain speakers who I think need a little push. I am still careful not to deprive the class of ownership.

Certainly, the Critique has definite value. Only the individual teacher can determine if it merits the time required away from a structured class. However, I would also add that teachers who do not employ the Critique should definitely use general evaluation sheets at least periodically to keep tabs on strengths and weakness as the students perceive them.

CHAPTER 10

Follow-up Writing

Brain research indicates the undeniable value of writing as a tool for moving information from short to long-term memory. Brain experts claim students retain about 70% of the information they write about in comparison to the 10% they retain from a lecture. The particular subject does not seem to matter; in other words, even in a math class, students retain far more when they write about the way they solve a problem. I know one high school whose football team comes into the computer lab immediately after each game to provide the players with a chance to write (and think) about the strengths and weaknesses of their performances. It would be a shame then, to pass on the opportunity for writing as a follow-up to a Seminar.

In addition to this obvious benefit, writing can accomplish three important goals:

1. It ensures that every student, even if he/she offers little in the actual Seminar, is intimately involved in the text and participates in analysis and evaluation of that text.

2. It allows the teacher the opportunity to emphasize a key point which may have been missed – without taking away student ownership—by giving a prompt which directly addresses that point.

3. It ensures that all students, both the inner and outer circle, are directly involved with the text.

An illustration of point three is warranted. I recently observed an Advanced Placement, U.S. History teacher using the Seminar to engage his students in two dialogues about Douglas MacArthur—one a biographical excerpt and one an autobiographical excerpt. He held two successive seminars using the inner and outer circle method. Comparisons were obvious, but without the writing he would have had no guarantee that both outer circles were paying attention to the inner circles' very important texts. His writing prompt could not have been answered without involvement: *"What major differences do the two texts contain?"*

Note: In this way, follow-up writings can also be used as exams. The above question would serve as an excellent test prompt with just a small addition: *"Write a conversation between the two. Be sure to use a minimum of three direct quotes from the readings themselves."* Or the teacher might ask, "*Do you think MacArthur would be likely to agree with the biographer's interpretation of history? Why?"* —if he wanted to see if students understood the full thrust of MacArthur's hubris. Indeed, there is no doubt that Dialogues can serve as great preparation for examinations.

CHAPTER 11

Prospective Seminar Topics

Although "readings" are undoubtedly the most common texts for Seminars, texts can come in all shapes and sizes. The purpose of this chapter is to show a variety of types of texts which I have seen used successfully in the classroom.

Two things are necessary to remember from basic brain research: *emotion* and *controversy* are two essentials for moving learning from the short-term to the long-term. Whenever possible, the teacher would be wise to choose topics which have emotional meaning and are controversial for a majority of students. It only makes sense that students will respond to subjects which have personal application (Sprenger).

The question of "pre-reading" or "night before" preparation often comes up. The teacher must use professional judgment in every case. Obviously, if the text is confusing and requires several readings, giving the students the text as a homework assignment first will yield benefits in the actual seminar the following day. The text mentioned below from *Angels and Demons* is one such text.

The classes and age levels listed below are not absolute. Certainly, many of these texts could be used at multiple levels and in multiple subject disciplines.

Readings

As stated above, "readings" are undoubtedly the most common texts. These might consist of a variety of passages and are readily available at every grade level:

1. Paragraphs from a novel or play: i.e. the paragraphs from *Angels and Demons* by Dan Brown where the Camerlengo, the spokesman for the Vatican, asks whether mankind has profited more from faith or science, just before the climax of the book.

2. Columns from a newspaper or magazine: i.e. Anna Quindlen's bi-weekly page at the back of *Newsweek.*

3. Passages from famous writings: i.e. the paragraph on "unjust laws" from Martin Luther King's "Letter from a Birmingham Jail."

4. Poetry

5. Published, controversial essays: i.e. Dr. Kevorkian on euthanasia.

Two sources have become somewhat famous for providing texts. Because I have no tie to either company, I will mention them only by name, but not provide addresses or websites. However, both are easy to find: *Touchstone* and *Paideia.*

Questions

A related reading, as described above, will almost certainly enrich the Seminar. However, the use of a single question, if the students can stay on task, is perfectly acceptable. The following are examples of single questions which could yield fruitful dialogue without forcing the teacher to seek out the "perfect text" to accomplish intended goals.

Do people who speak different languages live in different worlds? (Modern Language – high school)

Can all life be reduced to mathematics? (Mathematics – intermediate)

If history changes constantly with new found evidence, can the story relayed in history books ever be considered absolute truth? (History – upper elementary)

If cultures are destroyed or lives are lost, such as with the tragedies of the California missions, should this be considered progress? (History – grade 4)

Can experts determine "the beautiful" or is beauty in the eye of the beholder? (Art – intermediate)

Do male and female athletics deserve equal funding? (P.E. – high school)

Can a Democracy work in a country where the majority is uneducated? (Civics – grade 12)

Classic Art

Norman Rockwell's "The Problem We All Live With," portraying an African-American girl being escorted to school by the National Guard. (Social Studies – elementary)

Leonardo DaVinci's "Last Supper" using geometric shapes to show the symmetry of Renaissance art. (Math or Art – intermediate)

M.C. Escher's "Ascending and Descending" showing the mindless nonprogress of mankind. (Psychology – high school)

Problem Solving

The circle is divided into groups of two. A mathematical problem is posed for which a formula has not yet been proposed in class. After fifteen minutes, each group poses their method of solution. The dialogue focuses on which group's solution is the more correct and efficient. (Math – any level)

The question of a particular kind of pollution (i.e. water) is posed. The dialogue focuses on what might be the best solution. (Science – any level)

A short story is read in class, but stopped before the ending is given. The dialogue focuses on possible solutions for the protagonist's dilemma. (Language Arts – elementary)

Graphs and Diagrams

Venn Diagram: Students list who in the class has just a brother, who has just a sister, and who has both in the diagram. Students use language (more than, less than, equal to, etc.) to establish mathematical relationships. (Mathematics – grade 2)

Bar Graph: Given a bar graph showing countries and consumption of natural resources, the dialogue focuses on standard of living and the use of natural resources. (Cultural Geography – grade 9)

Pie Graph: Given a pie graph showing the percent of Republican voters from each religion who voted in a particular election, the dialogue focuses on why certain religions might cast their ballots a particular way. (U.S. History – grade 11)

Pictures

See Socratic Seminar Sample A – Chapter 8

Overhead photo of a village with all the necessary components – industry, homes, farms, etc.—to study what comprises a society. (Social Studies – grade 3)

Photo of the levies in New Orleans and the dikes in the Netherlands. Dialogue concerns potential effects of global warming. (Science – any grade)

Photo of U.S. Female soccer team winning the world cup in 1999. Dialogue focuses on why soccer is not the major sport in the U.S. (P.E. – any grade)

Objects

See Socratic Seminar Sample B – Chapter 8

Student-constructed Rain Forest on classroom wall with Floor, Understory, Canopy, Emergent Layer with animals in appropriate places. Dialogue focuses on why animals are best suited for different layers. (Science – Grade 2)

Clothing from several countries. Dialogue focuses on how fashion is an adaptation of the temperature and environment. (Geography – grade 8)

The Periodic Table. Could it be reorganized to be more effective? (Chemistry – grade 10)

CHAPTER 12

Socratic Seminar and Critical Thinking

The foundations of Critical Thinking—***open-mindedness*** and the ability to develop ***Counter-arguments***—also form the basis for the Socratic Seminar. Simply stated, a student is not thinking critically if he/she does not consider more than one point of view or alternative objectively. The critical thinker must climb beyond his/her bias and assumptions to choose the best solution or answer.

Therefore, we can safely state that participants in the Socratic Seminar are critical thinkers. Their main goal is to gain understanding of others' perspectives. They enter the seminar with an open mind, avoid falling into debate mode, and listen attentively to their fellow students' opinions. The participant knows full well that a change of mind is entirely possible. Each member, including the teacher, enters expecting to learn something new.

Thus, the marriage between the Seminar and Critical Thinking is, indeed, made in heaven. However, at this point we should take the time for several observations about other hallmarks of Critical Thinking within the realms of the generally accepted "Traits of Mind" and "Intellectual Standards" [as adapted from original lists from Richard Paul].

Traits of Mind

Independence

The participant frees himself from dependence on the belief systems of parents, religious persuasion, political leaning, etc.

Insight into egocentricity and ethnocentricity

The participant recognizes and dispels his/her own belief that he/she already has all the correct answers or that his/her own country or culture is always correct.

Fair-mindedness

The participant treats all viewpoints with an objective attempt to understand.

Humility

The participant willingly admits others' perspectives may be superior and hence reserves judgment until all viewpoints are heard.

Courage

The participant boldly ventures into new areas that may seem uncomfortable.

Perseverance

The participant does not give up on a text, but rather attempts to analyze it, with the help of classmates, bit by bit, until a clear picture is formed.

Curiosity

The participant is a seeker of new truth and expanded knowledge.

Responsibility

The participant brings only truth to the seminar, not attempting to use misinformation, such as invalid statistics.

Intellectual Standards

Relevant

The participant stays on topic and refers directly to the text.

Clear

The participant speaks clearly so that all members of the circle can hear without strain.

Precise

The participant speaks exactly to the point and eliminates "umm," "like a," etc.

Logical

The participant eliminates fallacious reasoning.

Consistent

The participant's logic is consistent, without ignoring certain rules when convenient or useful.

Significant

The participant attempts only to make comments which are insightful, avoiding any temptation to speak only for the sake of speaking.

Again, I cannot emphasize enough that the ability to analyze counter-arguments is the basis of critical thinking. And again, I cannot emphasize enough that seeking to understand these counter-arguments is the essence of the Socratic Seminar.

CHAPTER 13

A Final Word

One of the hallmarks of being a great educator, or being great in any walk of life for that matter, is the ability to change. Although many of us would like to stick to the tried and true methodologies by which we were taught, change is essential. Environments have changed dramatically, and along with them students' brains. Where walking through the snow six miles was once the major trauma of the day, students now may face twenty or more challenges before lunch every day. Where lecturing to straight rows with nailed-down desks was once the only way to teach, now "straight rows equal straight jackets."

And so, even if we believe we must cover X amount of material in X amount of time to have our students pass the X test, we must study brain research and accept that we must alter our strategies if we want information to be understood, processed, and committed to long-term memory—if we truly want to "educate" (which literally means "open up").

After thirty-seven years in the trenches, teaching the most gifted thinkers and the most reluctant learners, I promise you that the Socratic Seminar works. I guarantee it will bring you personal satisfaction and put smiles on the faces of your students. They will soon be begging for Seminar time.

Good luck! Have faith! The Socratic Seminar represents the future of education.

Works Cited

Adler, J. Mortimer. *The Paideia Proposal.* New York, NY: Simon and Schuster, 1998.

Bloom, Benjamin S. *Taxonomy of Educational Objectives.* Boston, MA: Allyn and Bacon, 1984.

Crusius, Timothy, and Carolyn Channell. *The Aims of Argument.* Mountain View, CA: Mayfield Publishing Company, 2000.

Klemke, E.D., and A. David Kline, and Robert Hollinger. *Philosophy: Contemporary Perspectives on Perennial Issues.* New York: St. Martins Press, 1994.

Paul, Richard. *Critical Thinking.* Santa Rosa, CA: Foundation for Critical Thinking, 1995.

Roberts, Terry, and Laura Billings. *The Paideia Classroom: Teaching for Understanding.* Larchmont, NY: Eye on Education. Inc. 1999.

Senge, Peter. *The Fifth discipline: the Art and Practice of the Business Organization.* New York: Currency – Doubleday. 1990.

Sprenger, Marilee. *Differentiation through Learning Styles and Memory.* Thousand Oaks, CA: Corwin Press, 2003.

Winchell, Peter Gryffon. *The Dialogue Game.* San Raphael, CA: The Invisible Press. 2006.

Acknowledgement

A personal thanks to two great principals: Dr. Duffy Clark, who brought the Socratic Seminar to Mission Viejo High School, and Mrs. Marilyn McDowell, who has allowed and encouraged its full implementation with students, teachers, and parents.